# Stratford-upon-Avon: an appreciation

# STRATFORD UPON AVON

## An appreciation

*by* LEVI FOX
*Director of the Shakespeare Birthplace Trust*

*A Jarrold Colour Publication, Norwich*

# Introduction

No town of comparable size enjoys such universal popularity as Stratford-upon-Avon, the birthplace of famous William Shakespeare. One of Warwickshire's oldest market towns, Stratford-upon-Avon possesses a peculiarly English character, derived from its unique heritage of natural setting, history, and literary association. Year by year the fame of its long-established Shakespeare Festival spreads as increasing numbers of visitors from all parts of the world come to enjoy the plays of the greatest dramatist of all time in the setting of his native town.

As a small town situated at the centre of an area of pleasant countryside, Stratford combines the atmosphere and tradition of the past with the activities and amenities of the present. Unspoiled by industrial development or a too-rapid expansion, the layout and

architecture of the town reflect the progress of its community life throughout the centuries and bear evidence to its prosperity at the present day. Outside the metropolis Stratford represents what Michael Drayton, another Warwickshire poet, called 'the heart of England'. The fascination is understandable.

The river and meadows, the streets and markets, the properties and gardens associated with the poet, the pastoral scenes and the country way of life combine with the survival of ancient custom and civic ceremony to perpetuate the background of Shakespeare's early environment. But Stratford is no mere repository of the past: in the Royal Shakespeare Theatre it has the 'workshop' of the living Shakespeare, while its growing recognition as an academic centre makes it increasingly a gathering-place for people of all nations.

*The Garden at Hall's Croft*

For centuries the Warwickshire Avon has commanded an importance and interest out of all proportion to its size. Surpassing in fame the Severn, whose other tributaries it dwarfs, this soft-flowing river abounds in historical and literary associations. Nowhere do natural beauty and the visible continuity of the English scene blend so effectively as in the countryside through which it winds its leisurely course, from historic Naseby in Northamptonshire to its junction with the Severn at Tewkesbury. Past ancient towns and villages, fine old mansions, great abbeys and beautiful churches, imposing castles and famous battlefields it flows. On every hand the peaceful panorama of the English countryside unfolds its undulating meadows, cultivated farms and scattered woodland, with its teeming plant and bird life, fruit and flowers, its country dwellers in their homes and fields.

*Early view of Clopton Bridge, published in 1795*

Stratford-upon-Avon is situated roughly midway along the Avon's course in the south-western corner of Warwickshire. The river broadens before the town into a broad and pleasant reach, unequalled in any other part of its course. On the one side, green meadows now preserved as open space stretch beyond its willow-fringed bank; on the other, the Royal Shakespeare Theatre dominates the Bancroft gardens and the unpretentious cottages of Waterside.

Two bridges span the river at this point: the historic stone bridge of Clopton fame which after nearly five centuries of constant use still carries all road traffic across the river; and a brick-built bridge, relic of an early nineteenth-century tramway scheme, which in retirement affords crossing for pedestrians. Standing on the tramway bridge and looking downstream, no one can fail to be impressed by the exceptional beauty of this scene: the quiet, slow-gliding waters; the graceful swans and little boats; the vista of meadow and gardens with their infinite shades of green; the

*The Clopton Bridge*

*Two bridges span the Avon at Stratford*

*Holy Trinity Church, Stratford*

over-hanging willows and scattered trees; in the background the imposing spire of Holy Trinity Church
—a rare gem in a priceless setting—towering gracefully
heavenwards; nearer, the coloured flower-boxes
perched on the terrace of the Royal Shakespeare
Theatre; and then, rising on a gentle slope, the ir-
regular shapes and lines of the buildings of the town.

From early days the river has powerfully influenced
the fortunes of this place. Prehistoric man made his
way along its valley; in Roman times a road or *stræt*
across its ford gave it the name of *Stratford*; Saxon
invaders settled and flourished here; from Domesday
at least its waters worked a mill which ground corn
for those who lived here; medieval rivercraft carried
wool and other produce downstream to Tewkesbury
and beyond, and later navigation schemes made it a
channel of high commerce; from time to time the
flooding of its waters exposed the Stratford townsfolk
to great danger and disaster, as for instance in 1588

*William Shakespeare*

—the year of the Spanish Armada—when a sudden rise in the river carried away all the hay in the Avon valley, breaking both ends of Stratford bridge, and leaving a trail of damage all along the river course; nowadays, the fishing, boating, and the charm of its unspoiled scenery afford recreation for city dwellers.

But it is not primarily the beauty of its Avon or the history and character of its town that makes Stratford famous. Its outstanding claim to universal attention is that William Shakespeare, the greatest dramatic genius of the English-speaking peoples, was born and died here. Writing in 1656, Sir William Dugdale, Warwickshire's distinguished antiquary, thought fit to remind his readers that 'one thing more, in reference to this antient town is observable, that it gave birth and sepulture to our late famous *Will. Shakspere*'. That reminder is no longer necessary, for Stratford is known as Shakespeare's town the world over, and as such has become one of Britain's greatest tourist assets.

*South-east prospect of Stratford, 1746*

# History

Of the antiquity of Stratford there is abundant archaeological and historical evidence. Though its beginnings are lost in obscurity, excavations have established that a Romano-British village flourished alongside the river upstream from Clopton Bridge from the early days of the Roman occupation until the beginning of the sixth century, when it was destroyed by the Saxons, who also settled here. Subsequently a small Saxon monastery established itself, probably near to the site of Holy Trinity Church, and by the time of the Norman Conquest Stratford comprised a small community of people, mostly engaged in tilling the land, who acknowledged the Bishop of Worcester as their lord.

Developments occurred during the twelfth century, which had a great influence on Stratford's early development. Realizing the natural advantages of its

*The Bancroft Gardens*

*The Market Cross*

river-crossing site, considerably enhanced by the building of a wooden bridge about this time, Bishop John
of Coutances secured for Stratford in 1196 the grant
of a weekly market and in 1214 King John granted a
three days' fair. Soon Stratford became a centre of
exchange, and a survey of 1251 indicates that in addi-
tion to those tilling the land, tradesmen, such as
carpenters, blacksmiths, millers, shoemakers, dyers,
coopers, and wheelwrights, were living here.

Stratford's importance as a town of markets and
fairs steadily increased during the Middle Ages; but
even so, it remained small and did not figure in the
events of national history. As part of an ecclesiastical
estate, Stratford did not attain independent borough
status and was never represented in Parliament. Nevertheless, its contacts with the outside world were not
negligible. Travellers and merchandise passing from
north to south crossed the Avon by its bridge; cloth
and wool from the prosperous city of Coventry passed

*Bridge Street*

*The Gild Chapel*

through on their way to Bristol and beyond; buyers came from distances to attend its fairs and the country people around frequented its markets.

Moreover, some of Stratford's sons left their town and rose to eminence, as did Shakespeare himself later: John de Stratford, who enlarged the Parish Church and established a college of priests near by, became Archbishop of Canterbury in Edward III's reign; his brother, Robert de Stratford, rose to be Bishop of Chichester; later, in Henry VII's reign, Hugh Clopton, a successful merchant, made his way to London and became Lord Mayor. He it was who built 'the great and sumptuose bridge'—so described half a century later—which from then to now has contributed powerfully to the prosperity of the town.

On the constitutional and social side the medieval history of Stratford is bound up with the existence and activities of the Gild of the Holy Cross. Founded in 1269, it had become by the fifteenth century a notable

*The Elizabethan Knott Garden at New Place*

*The Schoolroom, above the Gildhall, where Shakespeare may have been educated*

fraternity of brethren and sisters, with a county repu-
tation. Though primarily religious in its objects, in
course of time the gild virtually came to exercise the
powers of town government. Enriched by the gifts and
bequests of its members, it owned considerable properties in the town, the income from which maintained
priests in the Gild Chapel, paid a schoolmaster to
teach in its school, kept up almshouses for its aged
members, assisted the repair of the bridge, and made
possible various other kinds of social welfare work.

Stratford's gild was dissolved in 1547, leaving
behind it a fine tradition, substantial buildings, many
of which still survive, and records containing a wealth
of information about the medieval town and its
people. In its place, by virtue of a charter granted by
King Edward VI in 1553, the inhabitants were
incorporated under the name of the Bailiff (later
changed to Mayor) and burgesses of Stratford-upon-
Avon and vested with most of the gild's property and

*The Gild Chapel
from Scholars Lane*

*An early drawing of the Birthplace, 1769*

responsibilities. The Corporation's powers were further defined by charter in 1610, and the machinery of town government set up remained effective until the middle of the eighteenth century.

On the economic side Stratford still remained, in the words of Camden, writing in 1586, 'a proper little mercate town', depending for its prosperity on trade rather than manufacture. As a market for the supply of corn, seeds, malt, and country produce it had no equal for many miles around, whilst its horse sales attracted buyers and sellers from most of the Midland counties and especially from the Severn and Avon valleys. The chief local trade was malting, but during the reigns of Elizabeth I and James I the town became the centre of a flourishing glove-making trade. John Shakespeare, the poet's father, was a glover and whittawer. Cloth-making, which had been an important trade earlier, was by this time in decline.

*The kitchen and the 'baby-minder'*     During the seventeenth century Stratford became

*An 1821 engraving of Clopton House*

the scene of stirring events which link it with the story of English history. The Gunpowder Plot conspirators used Clopton House near by as one of their haunts; it was rented by Ambrose Rookwood and after Fawkes' arrest found to contain various Popish relics. During the Civil War the town experienced considerable military activity, though the townspeople were not enthusiastic supporters of either side. After the battle of Edgehill, fought near by, the Parliamentary garrison fell back on the town, which was occupied by the Royalists, only to be recaptured by the Parliamentary forces later. Stratford inevitably suffered loss: Clopton Bridge was damaged by military action; the Town Hall blew up due to the explosion of three barrels of gunpowder; the free quarter and plunder of troops impoverished many of the inhabitants.

It was in these troubled times, in 1643, that Queen Henrietta Maria, Charles I's queen, visited the town staying for three days at New Place, as the guest of

*The Avon and Holy
Trinity Church in
the early 1700s*

Susanna Hall, Shakespeare's elder daughter. The occasion was appropriately celebrated by bell-ringing and feasting.

Shortly afterwards, in 1672, a scheme for improving the navigability of the Avon, begun by William Sandys of Fladbury nearly forty years earlier and taken up by Yarranton and others later, was completed. The benefits to Stratford were great, for vessels of up to thirty tons burthen were thereby enabled to carry their cargoes thence direct, thus linking the rich-growing district round about with the coal and iron of Shropshire, the cloth of the middle Severn Valley, and the trade of Gloucester and Bristol. Quays were built near to the present Swan's Nest Hotel, and the town assumed the aspect of a small inland port. The Avon navigation continued on a diminishing scale until the middle of the last century. The canal reached Stratford in 1816 and in the 1820's a horse-drawn tramway was built to connect the wharves at Stratford with

*The Gower Memorial
overlooking the
canal basin
in the Bancroft Gardens*

*Anne Hathaway's Cottage in 1795*

Shipston-on-Stour and Moreton-in-Marsh.

In other respects, apart from its increasing popularity as the home of Shakespeare, the history of the town in the eighteenth and early nineteenth centuries has few outstanding features of interest. Earlier local govern-ment arrangements gradually broke down in the face of changing conditions, but Stratford's municipal life offers no evidence of the decadence and corruption found in many boroughs at this period. With the construction of the turnpike roads, an increased amount of traffic began to pass through the town, and by the early nineteenth century Stratford had become deeply involved in the coaching trade. In 1817, at least twenty-four main road coaches a day passed through on the route from London to Birmingham, Shrewsbury and Holyhead.

The coming of the railway in the 1850's and later of mechanical road transport altered all this. Indeed the last hundred years mark a momentous period in Strat-

*The Cottage and garden*

*The parlour, with
its 'courting-settl*

*The stone dovecote among the buildings behind the house*

ford's history. Widening appreciation of Shakespeare and Stratford's growing popularity as a place of recreation—the two are not necessarily connected—have with the aid of improved communications made Shakespeare's town pre-eminently a tourist centre. Hotels, restaurants, souvenir shops, and other amenities have been provided and the so-called 'tourist industry' now stands high in the list of local occupations.

Nevertheless, Stratford still maintains its original role of a market centre, providing facilities for the sale of produce and cattle from the surrounding countryside. Stratford also has a miscellany of small light industries, which include the manufacture of engineering and structural components; fruit canning; the making of road signs, light castings, and aluminium goods; various crafts associated with agriculture and market gardening; printing; and an extensive farmers' insurance business. A policy of enlightened self-interest has studied the practical interests of the local community whilst preserving the town's unique heritage.

*Middle Row, Bridge Street, at the end of the last century*

# The Town,
# Past and Present

From the point of view of layout and architecture, Stratford is a town of considerable interest and character, and visitors from the sixteenth century onwards have been struck by its appearance. As early as 1540, John Leland observed that the town was 'reasonably well builded of timber' and was impressed by the orderly plan of its 'very large streets'. He noted the Parish Church as 'a fair large piece of work', the Gild Chapel as a 'right goodly chapel' with the grammar school and almshouses adjoining, and Clopton Bridge, newly built with its fourteen stone arches. All these features, together with the plan of the central streets, still remain essentially unaltered.

Carl Philipp Moritz, who included Stratford in his

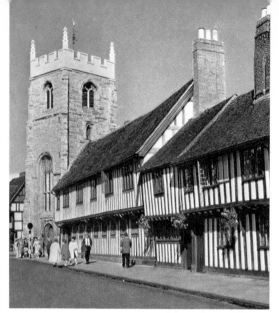

*The Almshouses and
the Grammar School*

travels in 1782, referred to the width of the Avon and
the 'row of neat, though humble cottages' ranged
along Waterside. 'These houses impressed me
strongly,' he wrote, 'with the idea of patriarchal simplicity and content.' Moncrieff's *Excursion* (1824), a
guide-book which enjoyed considerable popularity,
described Stratford as 'small, but handsome and airy'
and 'much more regular in its plan and buildings,
than the generality of towns of any antiquity'. It
contained 'many old houses, presenting curious speci-
mens of ancient architecture', while the modern buildings were 'spacious and well-built'. May's *Companion
Book*, published in 1827, added that 'clean brick and
tile, with fitting masonry' were also general, imparting
'an air of cleanliness and durability to the place'.

These impressions point to all the elements necessary
for appreciating the character of present-day Stratford.
Unspoiled by industry or the aftermath of a too-rapid
expansion, the layout and architecture of the town as

*Half-timbered buildings in Chapel Street*

a whole reflect the economic, social, and cultural background of community life here through the centuries. Within the compact framework of its ancient streets, many of whose names perpetuate their former rustic associations, are buildings of many styles belonging to all periods. The predominant architectural style is the picturesque half-timbered work associated with Elizabethan and Jacobean times. Hard by Stratford formerly stretched the Forest of Arden (used by Shakespeare as the setting for *As You Like It*), and it was accordingly timber, with a small amount of local stone, that provided the necessary building materials over a very long period. The result was a type of building which seems to strike a note of harmony with the surrounding Warwickshire countryside. Though there are some earlier, many of the surviving half-timbered buildings belong to a period of rebuilding following 1594 and 1595, two years when disastrous fires destroyed many houses in the central part of the town.

*Harvard House in High Stre built in 159*

*Chapel Street, circa 1810*

But Stratford is not entirely half-timbered. The eighteenth century saw considerable building activity: the quiet dignity and formal elegance of the frontages built at this time harmonize admirably with the background of earlier half-timbered work. The striking spire of Holy Trinity Church and the Town Hall with its finely proportioned ballroom both belong to this period, as also a number of brick and plaster frontages concealing genuinely older buildings.

The nineteenth century, too, added its contribution to the architectural quality of the town, not in any notable individual buildings (except perhaps for the first Shakespeare Memorial Theatre burned down in 1926), but rather in the inoffensive background provided by its varied structures of brick and tile, with occasional stucco work. The building now used as Barclays Bank (formerly a market hall) at the top of Bridge Street with its quaint clock tower may not rank as great architecture, but it is not in many ways an

*Holy Trinity Church*

undignified successor to the old market cross which
once graced its site. The same remarks apply, with
some exceptions, to the few twentieth-century buildings and adaptations in the town. The Royal Shakespeare Theatre, with its striking simplicity of plan and
design, can alone claim mention as an exceptionally
interesting example of pre-war architecture; the merits
of other buildings added at that time are on the whole
negative in the sense that, if they do not enhance the
general character of the town, they do not at any rate
spoil it. In post-war years, apart from individual
business premises, perhaps the rebuilding of Meer
Street has provided the best example of harmonizing
new with old, while the new Shakespeare Centre
adjacent to Shakespeare's Birthplace is a building of
unusually imaginative modern design.

Stratford, then, is a town where the continuous
contribution of the past, and its fusion with the
present, is visible materially and perceptible spiritually.

Its clean, unpretentious, natural, and typically English appearance is perhaps its greatest asset. Some find pleasure chiefly in its river scenes, the fine view from the Welcombe Hills, the wild beauty of Weir Brake or Hatton Rock, the flowered maze of the Knott Garden at New Place, or the arched avenue of spreading limes leading to the church; others enjoy the atmosphere of its ancient buildings and their associations, the rich cultural heritage of the Parish Church, the Gild Chapel, the Birthplace, Anne Hathaway's Cottage, Mary Arden's House, and all the treasures they contain; to the country people round about its shopping facilities, its busy cattle market on Tuesdays, its function as a market town serving their needs, still have the strongest appeal; finally, and by no means least, lovers of the drama from the four corners of the world enjoy with reverence and delight the comfort and intimacy of the Royal Shakespeare Theatre, where Shakespeare himself reigns supreme.

*An early view of Harvard House*

# The Stratfordian

The designation of Stratfordian should not be lightly or indiscriminately applied to all who live in Stratford. For of its small population there are roughly three to one who are not natives of the place; and of these 'outsiders' hardly half have not lived here sufficiently long to have been adopted as Stratfordians.

Living in an essentially small town, Stratfordians display most of the characteristics encountered in a small community. They know each other and freely exchange news and views about their fellows and happenings in the town. From this it must not be inferred that Stratford is more prone to gossip than any other place of similar size; it is merely that

*Henley Street before 1850*

Stratfordians evince a lively intelligence and mutual interest in each other's affairs.

The new-comer may at first form the opinion that Stratfordians are exclusive and not very friendly. Nothing could be more mistaken, for once the ice has been broken, they are large-hearted people, very human and generous in their hospitality. It is easy to misjudge them, as did Anthony Langston, Town Clerk in 1617, who threw up his office in despair soon after his election, 'finding so much jealous heart-burning amongst the best of the borough, and being out of all hope of purification'. He later withdrew his resignation, with the approval of those whom he had condemned, finding they were not so bad after all.

The Stratfordian is inevitably conservative by nature. He is not averse to new ideas as such but drastic change is distasteful to him. Many things are done in Shakespeare's town in a particular manner, not because it is the best or most effective way of

*Anne Hathaway's Cottage and garden*

doing them, but because that is how they have always been done. 'The people of Stratford', it was said half a century ago, 'are like its houses, still partly of an ancient style.' Yet though perhaps casual on the surface, they are none the less sensible, practical folk, good at business, and not easily taken in.

The Stratfordian has a wider experience of people than most small town dwellers. He is at home conversing with the country folk who come in on market days, but is accustomed to the sound of many foreign tongues and accents and the sight of varied national costumes in his shops and streets. To all he shows a courtesy which visitors are quick to note.

In one sense Stratford belongs to the Stratfordian only. He is extremely proud of his ancient borough town, its customs, traditions, and historic buildings. The average burgess may have surprisingly little knowledge of the history of the place or of Shakespeare; but he has a consciousness of his historic environment,

*Folk dancers in the orchard*

takes a lively interest in local affairs, and is quick to resent interference from outside. In no place is there a finer tradition of public service.

His local pride is linked with an instinct for ancient custom, civic ceremony, and traditional pageantry. Anyone who has seen the Stratford Mop on 12 October—survival of the annual hiring fair—can appreciate his love of traditional celebration, even though the occasion has now lost its original significance; and the same is true of the festivities on Shakespeare's Birthday.

Stratford-upon-Avon, indeed, is not unworthy of the genius who crowned her with glory. 'I find it as interesting and alive,' wrote one who knew and appreciated more of Stratford's material and spiritual heritage than most, 'as rich in the clash of thought and character, as full of kind and wise if somewhat quaint humanity, as once, before I had studied it and merely accepted tradition and opinion, I supposed it to be mean and commonplace.'

*The floral procession in Church Street, celebrating Shakespeare's birthday*

*A pine-wood carving of Shakespeare
of late eighteenth-century date*

# Shakespeare and Stratford

William Shakespeare, Stratford's greatest son, was born in the house preserved as his Birthplace in Henley Street on or about 23 April 1564, and the record of his baptism is entered in the register of the Parish Church. His mother, Mary Arden, was the daughter of Robert Arden, a substantial yeoman farmer of Wilmcote; his father, John Shakespeare, formerly of Snitterfield, a glover and whittawer by trade who did business as a wool-dealer. William was the eldest son and third child of the marriage, and at the time of his birth John Shakespeare was a prosperous, respected tradesman, who took an active part in municipal affairs and held the office of Bailiff of the town in 1568.

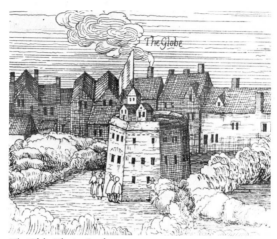

The Globe Theatre, London,
where many of Shakespeare's
plays were performed

Of William's childhood practically nothing is known. There is every reason to believe that he attended the local grammar school, and very probably saw some of the plays produced by the companies of travelling actors who were officially welcomed in Stratford when he was a boy. When little over eighteen he married Anne Hathaway of Shottery, and shortly afterwards, for reasons not definitely known, left Stratford. Within a short time he can be traced in London, first as an actor and then as a reviser and writer of plays. By 1592 his contemporaries were excited and indignant about the quality and popularity of his work, and his association with companies of players and the production of his plays can be substantiated from this time onwards.

Shakespeare's success as a playwright and a partner in theatrical ventures brought him wealth, some of which he used to purchase property in London and Stratford. In 1597 he bought New Place, the principal

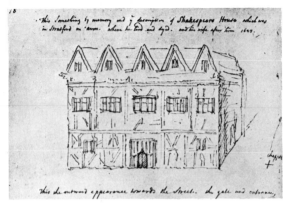

*18*

· This Something by memory and y description of Shakespeare House which was in Stratford on 'Avon. where he lived and dyd. and his wife after him 1623:

this the outward appearance towards the Street. the gate and entrance,

*The earliest surviving drawing of New Place*

house in his native town, and to this he retired in 1610 to live with his family and friends. Tradition and his will show that he lived upon friendly terms with the leading townsmen and gentry of the neighbourhood. He died on 23 April 1616 at the age of fifty-two and was buried in the chancel of the Parish Church.

Within less than twenty years Stratford was already recognized as 'a Towne most remarkeable for the birth of famous William Shakespeare', and during the next century a number of writers recorded Shakespearian traditions and made copies of the inscription on the poet's tomb. By the middle of the eighteenth century visitors wishing to see Shakespeare's mulberry tree at New Place, said to have been planted by the poet himself, had become so numerous as to cause annoyance to the then owner of the property, Reverend Francis Gastrell, who in consequence had the tree cut down in 1756. When three years later he caused the house itself to be demolished, local indignation rose to such

*Shakespeare's monument in Holy Trinity Church*

*The octagonal Jubilee Amphitheatre erected for the Festival*

heights that he was compelled to quit the town
'amidst the rage and curses of its inhabitants'.

But it was the widely-publicized Shakespearian
Festival of 1769, organized by the famous actor David
Garrick, which gave the real impetus to Stratford's
rising popularity as the shrine of literary pilgrimage.
A magnificent octagonal amphitheatre was erected on
the Bancroft and the whole town decorated and illuminated in a brilliant manner. Garrick's recitation of
his Shakespearian Ode with Arne's music marked
the highlight of the programme, which included the
firing of cannons, public breakfasts, concerts,
masquerade and ball, serenades, processions, fireworks, horse-racing on Shottery meadow, and the
like—everything except, paradoxically enough, the
performance of a Shakespearian play.

The continued recognition of the buildings associated with Shakespeare was assured from this time.
Walpole, who visited the Birthplace in 1777, describes

*The programme for Stratford*
*first Shakespeare Festiv.*
*in 176*

# FIRST DAY,

*Wednesday*, the 6th of *SEPTEMBER*,

# Shakeſpeare's Jubilee.

The STEWARD of the JUBILEE begs Leave to inform the COMPANY,
that at Nine o'Clock will be

# A PUBLIC BREAKFAST

## At the TOWN-HALL:

Thence to proceed to the CHURCH to hear

## The ORATORIO of *JUDITH,*

Which will begin exactly at ELEVEN.

From Church will be a full CHORUS of VOCAL and INSTRUMFNTAL
MUSIC to the AMPHITHEATRE; where, at Three o'Clock, will be

## An ORDINARY for Gentlemen and Ladies.

About Five o'Clock, a Collection of NEW SONGS, BALLADS, ROUNDELAYS,
CATCHES, GLEES, &c. will be performed in the AMPHITHEATRE; after
which the Company is defired to prepare for the BALL, which will
begin exactly at Nine, with NEW MINUETS, (compoſed for the Occaſion)
and played by the whole Band.

The SECOND DAY'S ENTERTAINMENTS will be publiſhed To-morrow.

*N. B.* As the PUBLIC BREAKFASTS and ORDINARIES are intended for
thoſe Ladies and Gentlemen who have taken the Guinea Tickets, no Per-
ſon can be admitted without firſt ſhewing ſuch Ticket. Should there be
Room for more than the Proprietors of thoſe Tickets, Ladies and
Gentlemen will be admitted to the ORATORIO and FIREWORKS, at *Five
Shillings* each; and to the DEDICATION, ODE, and BALL, at *Half a
Guinea* each.

\*₊\* The STEWARD hopes that the Admirers of *Shakeſpeare*, will, upon
this Occaſion, wear the Favors which are called the *Shakeſpeare Favors.*

☞ As many Ladies have complained of the Fatigue they ſhall undergo,
if the Ball and Maſquerade are on two ſucceſſive Nights, there will
be only the FIREWORKS on *Thurſday* Night, and the MASQUERADE on
*Friday* Night, the 8th Inſt. which will conclude the Entertainments of
the Jubilee.

*The foundations of New Place*

how he was shown Shakespeare's chair, which had been 'pretty much cut by different visitors', a statement illuminated by the Hon. John Byng, who says in his diary in 1785 that he bought 'a slice of the chair equal to the size of a tobacco stopper'. Washington Irving gives in his *Sketch Book* an amusing list of the spurious relics which he saw exhibited in the house in 1815, including 'the shattered stock of the very matchlock with which Shakespeare shot the deer . . . his tobacco box . . . the sword also with which he played Hamlet . . . '. This was shameless exploitation, and when Shakespeare's house was offered for sale in 1847 public opinion was sufficiently strong to ensure its purchase for preservation as a national memorial.

Since that time the property has been administered by the Shakespeare Birthplace Trust, which has also acquired for preservation Anne Hathaway's Cottage, the early home of Shakespeare's wife; New

*The back of
Mary Arden's House*

Place, where Shakespeare lived in retirement and died; Mary Arden's House, the home of the poet's mother; and Hall's Croft, the home of Shakespeare's daughter Susanna and Dr John Hall. At the same time the Birthplace Trust has built up museum, library, and record collections containing a great wealth of source material of importance to scholars.

The modern cult of Shakespeare at Stratford also owes much to the work of the Royal Shakespeare Theatre. Although Shakespeare was frequently performed in Stratford during the eighteenth century— John Ward's *Othello* in 1746 is the earliest production recorded—it was not until 1827 that the town had its first Shakespearian theatre in Chapel Lane. Then in 1874, ten years after the successful tercentenary celebrations, the Shakespeare Memorial Association came into existence. The enthusiasm and generosity of its founder, Charles Edward Flower, knew no bounds, and in 1879 the old Shakespeare Memorial Theatre,

*The river frontage of
the Royal Shakespeare Theatre*

the predecessor of the present building, was opened.
From then to the present, Stratford has had a Festival
of Shakespeare's plays each year. Originally lasting
only a few weeks, the Shakespeare season now extends
for over eight months of the year, linking Stratford with
the most eminent actors and actresses of the day and
with an ever-increasing circle of Shakespeare lovers.

In post-war years Stratford companies have visited
Australia, New Zealand, Germany, Holland, France,
Belgium, Austria, Switzerland, Denmark, Norway,
Yugoslavia, Poland, Russia, Japan, Canada and the
United States. The theatre has now a permanent
London home in the Aldwych Theatre.

Since the war there have also been important
developments affecting the academic aspect of Shakespearian appreciation in Stratford-upon-Avon. Each
season courses of study and lectures are arranged. The
Festival Club at Hall's Croft provides a cultural and
social centre. A poetry festival, musical programme,

*Flowers decorate Shakespeare's grave in Holy Trinity Church on the anniversary of his birth*

and exhibitions are now held each year. The theatre has its own picture gallery, and in the new Shakespeare Centre, built by the Birthplace Trustees to commemorate the 400th anniversary of Shakespeare's birth, the resources of the Theatre and Birthplace libraries are freely available to students of all nations.

Last, but no means least, Stratford arranges celebrations in honour of the poet's birth on St George's Day, 23 April, each year, which are attended by official representatives of the nations of the world. From small beginnings, designed to give local people an opportunity to honour the memory of their great townsman, these celebrations have now assumed the proportions of an international occasion absolutely unique in its purpose and attraction. The luncheon with its traditional toasts, the ceremonial unfurling of the flags of the nations, and the floral procession from the Birthplace to the poet's tomb are but symbols of a universal recognition of the enduring genius of the poet.

# Principal Features of Interest

CLOPTON BRIDGE *Good example of a stone bridge of four-teen arches, built at the end of the fifteenth century by Hugh Clopton, a native of the town who became Lord Mayor of London.*

ROYAL SHAKESPEARE THEATRE *This stern, brick-built theatre was erected in 1932 to the design of Miss Elizabeth Scott, cousin of the architect of Liverpool Cathedral, to replace an earlier building (of which the library and art gallery adjoining formed part) built in 1879 and destroyed by fire in 1926. Built and endowed largely by subscriptions from overseas, particularly from America.*

SHAKESPEARE'S STATUE IN THE BANCROFT GARDENS *This statue of Shakespeare, the work of Lord Ronald Sutherland Gower, was presented to the town in 1888. The small figures are Hamlet, Lady Macbeth, Falstaff, and Prince Hal, symbolizing philosophy, tragedy, comedy, and history.*

SHAKESPEARE'S BIRTHPLACE *The half-timbered house where Shakespeare was born in 1564, and spent his early years. Part of the building is furnished and part accommodates a unique collection of books, manuscripts, pictures, and objects illustrative of the life, times, and works of the poet. The garden contains trees, plants, and flowers mentioned in Shakespeare's plays and poems. The property was purchased as a national memorial to the poet in 1847. Immediately adjacent, overlooking the Birthplace garden, is the Shakespeare Centre, built to commemorate the 400th anniversary of Shakespeare's birth.*

SHAKESPEARE CENTRE *A fine modern building of striking design providing a good illustration of the skilful use of traditional materials. Overlooking the Birthplace garden it serves as the headquarters of the Shakespeare Birthplace Trust. Inside may be seen artistic embellishments of unusual interest.*

HARVARD HOUSE *Of special interest to Americans. The maiden home of Katherine Rogers, mother of John Harvard, the founder of the great American University which bears his name. Built in 1596, this building is an outstanding specimen of late Elizabethan timberwork. Adjoining is the Garrick Inn and a picturesque Elizabethan building called the Old Tudor House.*

TOWN HALL *Dedicated to the memory of Shakespeare by the famous actor, David Garrick, in 1769, the Town Hall is a building of considerable dignity and charm. It is the scene of town council meetings and many varied local activities.*

SHRIEVE'S HOUSE *Unusually lofty, half-timbered house, the home of William Rogers, a popular figure in Shakespeare's day.*

SHAKESPEARE HOTEL *One of Stratford's famous hostelries, striking for its picturesque gables and jettied upper stories.*

NEW PLACE *Here are preserved the foundations of New Place, the house where Shakespeare spent his retirement and died in 1616. The entrance is through New Place Museum, formerly the home of Thomas Nash, who married Shakespeare's granddaughter, Elizabeth Hall, and now a museum of local history, archaeology, and Shakespearian exhibits. Here also may be seen an Elizabethan Knott Garden and the Great Garden of New Place.*

FALCON HOTEL *Impressive half-timbered building of late fifteenth-century date, used as an inn since the middle of the seventeenth century.*

GILD CHAPEL *Originally founded in 1269 for the use of the members of the Gild of the Holy Cross. The chapel was considerably altered in 1450 and the present nave, tower, and porch were added at the end of the fifteenth century. Inside may be seen the remains of a remarkable series of medieval wall-paintings.*

GRAMMAR SCHOOL AND ALMHOUSES *An extraordinarily fine range of half-timbered buildings erected by the Gild of the Holy Cross in the fifteenth century. It was in the large schoolroom on the first floor that it is believed Shakespeare was educated, while in the Gildhall below he probably saw performances by travelling players. The almshouses adjoining still fulfil their original function of providing homes for twenty-four aged people.*

SHAKESPEARE INSTITUTE *A pleasing, early eighteenth-century building, formerly the home of the novelist, Marie Corelli, which is now maintained as the Shakespeare Institute by the University of Birmingham.*

HALL'S CROFT *A fine Tudor town house in Old Town, it was the home of Shakespeare's daughter Susanna and her husband, Dr John Hall. Apart from its associations Hall's Croft is a building of outstanding character, possessing many interesting architectural features and a spacious walled garden. It accommodates a number of special attractions, including period rooms containing rare furniture, and an Elizabethan dispensary with exhibits relating to Dr John Hall.*

HOLY TRINITY CHURCH *Exceptionally beautiful, well-proportioned Parish Church, world famous as the church where Shakespeare was baptized and buried. An epitome of English ecclesiastical styles; the church is notable for a number of interesting features, including Shakespeare's monument and gravestone in the chancel.*

ROTHER MARKET *Scene of Stratford's weekly market held on Friday, and formerly of its cattle market. The American Fountain, erected in 1887, is overlooked by the White Swan Hotel, which was in use as a tavern in Shakespeare's time.*

MASON'S COURT *Unique local specimen of early fifteenth-century domestic architecture.*

ANNE HATHAWAY'S COTTAGE *This cottage, with its lovely garden and orchard, was the early home of Shakespeare's wife, Anne Hathaway, and of the Hathaway family. The building, part of which dates from the fifteenth century, has a thatched roof and walls of timber-framing and abounds in interesting architectural features. Inside the Cottage are preserved original Hathaway furniture and relics, including a fine Elizabethan bedstead.*

MARY ARDEN'S HOUSE *The home of Shakespeare's mother, Mary Arden. Situated at Wilmcote, in typical Warwickshire country, this property is a fine example of a farmstead of Tudor date, built of close-timbered oak beams and local stone. The house is furnished in period style and the barns serve as a museum for old Warwickshire agricultural implements and bygones.*

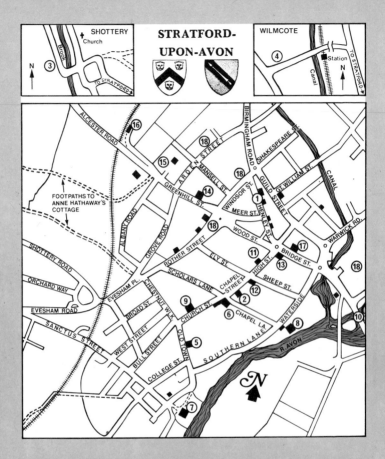

1 Shakespeare's Birthplace, Shakespeare Centre; 2 New Place and Gardens; 3 Anne Hathaway's Cottage; 4 Mary Arden's House; 5 Hall's Croft; 6 Gild Chapel and Grammar School; 7 Holy Trinity Church; 8 Royal Shakespeare Theatre; 9 Shakespeare Institute; 10 Clopton Bridge; 11 Harvard House; 12 Town Hall; 13 Information Centre; 14 Cinema; 15 Hospital; 16 Railway Station; 17 General Post Office; 18 Car Parks

The publishers gratefully acknowledge the courtesy of the Shakespeare Birthplace Trust for permission to reproduce illustrations of the Shakespearian properties

85306 658 2

© 1976 JARROLD COLOUR PUBLICATIONS, NORWICH

PRINTED IN GREAT BRITAIN BY

JARROLD AND SONS LTD, NORWICH 176